EXPLORING HI-TECH JOBS

Hi-Tech Jobs in VIDEO GAMING

Leanne Currie-McGhee

San Diego, CA

© 2024 ReferencePoint Press, Inc.
Printed in the United States

For more information, contact:
ReferencePoint Press, Inc.
PO Box 27779
San Diego, CA 92198
www.ReferencePointPress.com

ALL RIGHTS RESERVED.
No part of this work covered by the copyright hereon may be reproduced or used in any form or by any means—graphic, electronic, or mechanical, including photocopying, recording, taping, web distribution, or information storage retrieval systems—without the written permission of the publisher.

LIBRARY OF CONGRESS CATALOGING-IN-PUBLICATION DATA

Names: Currie-McGhee, L. K. (Leanne K.), author.
Title: Hi-tech jobs in video gaming / by Leanne Currie-McGhee.
Description: San Diego, CA : ReferencePoint Press, Inc., 2024. | Series: Exploring hi-tech jobs | Includes bibliographical references and index.
Identifiers: LCCN 2023026587 (print) | LCCN 2023026588 (ebook) | ISBN 9781678207021 (library binding) | ISBN 9781678207038 (ebook)
Subjects: LCSH: Video games--Design--Vocational guidance--Juvenile | Video games--Programming--Vocational guidance--Juvenile literature. | Video games industry--Vocational guidance--Juvenile literature.
Classification: LCC GV1469.3 .C87 2024 (print) | LCC GV1469.3 (ebook) | DDC 794.8--dc23/eng/20230809
LC record available at https://lccn.loc.gov/2023026587
LC ebook record available at https://lccn.loc.gov/2023026588

Contents

Introduction: The Future Is Now	4
Video Game Developer	7
Programmer	15
Audio Engineer	23
Game Animator	31
VR Game Designer	39
UI Designer	47
Source Notes	54
Interview with a UI/UX Designer	56
Other Jobs in Video Gaming	58
Index	59
Picture Credits	63
About the Author	64

Introduction: The Future Is Now

Sam Porter Bridges is searching for shelter. As deadly acid rain falls from the clouds, he seeks shelter for himself and the packages he carries. Without them, America cannot be saved. Sam is the main character in designer Hideo Kojima's video game, *Death Stranding*. The player's job is to control Sam and deliver his crucial supplies to isolated outposts of humanity. Delivering needed goods and reconnecting disparate communities is the player's goal in the postapocalyptic landscape of the game world. Kojima wants his players not only to become immersed in the game when undertaking Sam's mission but also to understand the relevance of the game's message in their own lives. "I want to create an experience in the game that people can use in the real world, like thinking about how we connect,"[1] explains Kojima.

As a game designer, Kojima brings a story and adventure to life for people to experience through play. Today's video games, like *Death Stranding*, are often visually detailed, with intricate storylines and major character development. Those involved in the creation of these complex games are typically passionate about gaming. And they are usually technically and creatively talented.

A Growing Industry

Video games are the leading form of entertainment in the United States: over 215 million people play them, according to the Entertainment Software Association. The popularity of these games protects them from the effects of inflation. Even as game prices rose in 2021, people continued to purchase them. Consequently, eight of the thirteen main gaming publishers saw an increase in revenues from 2021 to 2022. With such a high consumer demand, video game companies need more talent to perform the intricate and labor-intensive work of putting an entire game together. For many games, this work requires skills such as script writing, coding, acting, graphic design, music programming, and playtesting. Therefore, career opportunities in the field are many and varied.

The growth of the video game market has ensured that many occupations within the field provide stable livelihoods. "Recently, the video game industry became one of the largest industries in the world," asserts Dakota Vincent, a developer at Future House Studios. "For the last couple of decades, it has become more mainstream, and demand has gotten larger, ultimately leading to more jobs and job security for people working within the industry or wanting to be a part of it."[2]

A Leader in Technological Advances

Video games get better in terms of graphics, player capabilities, characters, and sounds each year, so there is a constant push to develop games that are more advanced. Those working within the field are on the forefront of technological innovation, learning skills that can have diverse applications beyond game design. For example, virtual reality (VR) teaches designers to create 3-D environments that players access via headsets and controllers. VR is still a niche market, but the gaming industry is pushing the limits of this immersive technology and providing blueprints for other fields—such as architecture, health care, automotive, and aerospace—to incorporate into their practices.

Another area of advancement is digital streaming, which allows people to play a live game with others on different devices—such as a console, smartphone, or laptop—over the internet. The games are stored in the "cloud," another name for the internet and its ability to store, retrieve, and operate programs from servers, powerful computer software dedicated to these functions. Many businesses use cloud-based services, and gaming is helping expand the reach and capabilities of the internet.

The Art of Creating and Designing

While possessing computer skills and an understanding of the technology involved in bringing games to life are important for many facets of game design, creators also need imagination. And almost every aspect of game design—from programming to testing—has a creative element. Duygu Cakmak is currently a project technical director at Creative Assembly, a gaming studio. She has found creativity to be an integral part of her career. "One of the biggest misconceptions around programming as a discipline is that it is not creative," explains Cakmak. "This is far from the truth—there are many ways to solve different problems and creativity is a key part of finding the right solutions. The consideration that goes into designing systems and features from the ground-up can be a form of art in and of itself."[3] It is successful translation of creativity into entertaining products that makes video gameplay exciting for legions of fans.

Careers in gaming are about that excitement. Designers love to develop and utilize new technologies to advance gameplay. They also share the public's anticipation for the next big title, and they take pride in the products that inspire loyal fans. If you love to game and are fascinated by the technological and artistic aspects of the games you play, you might find a rewarding career in this hi-tech field.

Video Game Developer

What Does a Video Game Developer Do?

Catt Small loved gaming as she grew up. She even taught herself how to code to bring some of her own game ideas to life. Following the path of a video game developer as a career has allowed her to maintain her passion as an adult. Small is the developer of *SweetXheart*, a story-driven, single-player game in which the user becomes Kara, a nineteen-year-old Black girl from the Bronx who attends an art college and interns at a tech company. Over five in-game days of going to school and work—as well as interacting with people in Kara's life—players get a feel for the stresses and experiences that a Black woman confronts when struggling to succeed. "There were parts in this game about harassment because being a Black woman in New York City, you experience a fair amount of street harassment. A man actually told me that he was not going to harass women or catcall women anymore after playing the game,"[4] Small explains. Her game is small and runs on a browser, but it has a sizable emotional impact on players and gets them thinking.

A Few Facts

Number of Jobs
About 1.62 million software developers in 2021

Pay
Median annual salary of $74,838

Educational Requirements
Bachelor's degree in video game design or any computer science field preferred

Personal Qualities
Creative, analytical, detail oriented

Work Settings
Indoors, in an office setting

Future Job Outlook
Growth rate of 25 percent through 2031

Get Help Building Your Skills

"There are scholarships, there are lots of programs that usually offer [video game development] lessons for free. I know there's Code Coven, I know Black Voices in Gaming is a thing, I know the Game Devs of Color Expo is a thing. You do not have to go through everything alone. There are communities out there that can help. . . . What matters is your experience and your knowledge working on games. Your portfolio can speak for itself."

—Geneva Heyward, game developer

Quoted in Brianna Scott, "The Number of Black Video Game Developers Is Small, but Strong," NPR, March 20, 2023. www.npr.org.

Video game developers like Small are the ones who turn a clever game idea into a reality. They often see a game through its development, from concept to entering the market. For those at larger companies, developers might only be responsible for specific stages in the production chain. In the beginning, developers can be part of the concept and design phases, generating ideas about what type of game it should be (such as racing, first-person shooter, or survival), the plot of the game, and its overall look and mechanics. This is especially true for small companies or games designed by one individual.

In larger companies, developers are part of a team. Once the production begins, developers are often the liaison between designers and programmers. Developers help ensure the programmers understand and can execute the designers' plans and that the designers understand the capabilities and limitations of the programmers' tools. Video game developers may manage coders or even help code the visual elements, play structure, and other features of the game. Developers often are involved in the testing of the game to ensure it performs well on the different platforms, and they oversee the debugging of any problems. At the end of the development, they are continually working to resolve any lingering problems with gameplay or performance.

A Typical Workday

For independent developers, those who develop their own games, a workday is filled with many tasks because they oversee all life stages of development. Neil Jones develops and markets his own games, so he is active in each stage. He creates an initial design document detailing the game's mechanics, flow, characters, plot, setting, visuals, and more. Once complete, his days may be divided between creating the art (using software such as Figma for drawing or Maya for animation), importing these designs into a game engine such as Unity or Unreal, and then building the game in the engine. He uses the preset components of the game engine—or might manually code within it—to structure the game. To create a game soundtrack, he might likewise use sounds within the engine and import his own musical score.

As the sole developer, he also must set aside time to analyze the market to sell the game. Jones says:

> You sit down and you code or you do art. In the larger scheme of things . . . developers have to deal with . . . not only sitting down and making the game, making sure the game is fun, but we have to worry about what other games are similar to our game. How can we stand out? How can you market the game? You have to make marketing materials. You have to do the sound effects in music.[5]

Education and Training

The key to becoming a game developer is gaining experience in designing, programming, and testing games. A formal education in game development or a related field will assist in building a game development career. Several game development and publishing companies look for candidates with a bachelor's degree in computer science or a related field, and more universities are offering game development and design as a major. Companies will also consider a person who has obtained skills through certificate programs. Schools such as the University of Washington, Harvard University, and Full Sail University offer professional certificate programs in game development, which take less than a year to acquire.

Many companies also look at practical experience, especially if you can demonstrate your skills through video games you have solely developed. You must show that you understand and are able to work with popular game engines that provide a framework for game development. Demonstrating programming skills—which are needed to add unique visuals, features, and details to the game—is also helpful. Whether through schooling or practical experience, developers should learn programming in C++ and C# because they will either be coding or overseeing others who are coding in these computer languages.

Skills and Personality

While game developers need technical skills such as programming and game engine knowledge, they must also have the drive to continually learn. There are new technical advancements in game design, up-and-coming program languages, and different gaming platforms that require developers to add to or modify their games. Staying up-to-date with changes in the field and its technology is important in order to ensure that your product will find a place in the market.

Being able to communicate, verbally and in writing, allows a game developer to interact with designers, programmers, testers, and anyone else involved in game development. Since a developer often oversees a portion or even all of game development, these individuals must ensure that team members understand what is needed of them to meet established goals and deadlines. It is also important to communicate success along the way by celebrating milestones in the development process.

Some video game developers work on all the different stages of game development. Others take on more specific tasks, including coding visual elements, play structure, and other features.

To be a game developer, you must be detail oriented. Games need to work without errors, and all aspects, from game logic to the soundtrack, must interact with each other seamlessly. Game developers are often imaginative people; either they are the sole creator or they play a key part in devising the game's primary concept. Creating a video game that is interesting and attractive to players requires the ability to think of unique ideas for its plot, mechanics, and characters.

Working Conditions

For the most part, game developers work at a desk, indoors on their computer, using the latest hardware and software technology. Typically, they have several monitors, headphones, and microphones. Aside from working at the computer, their day might include meetings with designers and programmers if they are part of a team.

Diversity Matters

"It's become incredibly important for me to work at studios that actively strive to include more diverse representation in their character designs and stories. At Amazon Games, I get to directly influence and shape the guiding principles and tenets of my game to ensure that it features authentic stories and inclusive experiences. During my time at Riot Games, I helped run and organize the 'Play like a Woman' initiative, which was an internal event that encouraged Rioters to build empathy by temporarily changing their [avatar] names to be more traditionally feminine facing. We interviewed several female-identifying developers, asking them to share more broadly their gaming experiences."

—Morgan Ling, game developer at Amazon

Morgan Ling, "Life & Work with Morgan Ling," Voyage LA, March 27, 2023. http://voyagela.com.

How busy a person is during the day depends on the stage of a game's development. The closer the deadlines are, the more intense the workload is. "I've also slogged through the 90-hour work weeks trying to get an unreasonable product done in time to meet an unreasonable deadline. Although my stimulant of choice wasn't energy drinks, it was a combination of strong black coffee and speed metal turned up way too loud in my headphones,"[6] explains Jason W. Bay, a veteran in the video gaming field who has worked as a developer.

Bay explains that the work environment within a gaming company is generally fun because the people enjoy interacting and talking about games. The staff members can still get stressed, as Bay mentions, but the office environment usually tolerates playful ways to take breaks. "That's why you're definitely going to find action figures, LEGOs, Nerf guns, remote-controlled drones, and other 'toys for grown-ups' in any game studio you walk into," Bay says. "It's how the relatively well-paid game developers express their interests, and how they blow off steam during crunch time."[7]

Employers and Earnings

Employers of video game developers range from large scale companies such as Activision Blizzard, Nintendo, and Valve Corporation to smaller, independent companies such as Askiisoft and Blendo Games. Also, game developers may freelance and create and sell their own games, although often they will need to work a full- or part-time job separately until they earn enough income from their own games.

According to the 2021 Developer Satisfaction Survey, conducted by the International Game Developers Association, 63 percent of full-time developers reported earning more than $50,000 per year. The job site Glassdoor shows a larger number—$74,838 average base pay—for game developers in the United States as of October 2022. The larger companies often pay much better, and developers who have more experience and take on lead roles in game production can earn six-figure salaries.

Future Outlook

The global gaming industry is bright, with predicted earnings of $321 billion in 2026, up from $235.7 billion in 2022, according to PricewaterhouseCoopers's Global Entertainment & Media Outlook. Given such expectations, all careers in the gaming industry will likely see growth. According to the Bureau of Labor Statistics, the job growth rate for game developers is 25 percent through 2031. If you are interested in using your skills to build a game from start to finish, this is a career to consider.

Find Out More

Game Developer

www.gamedeveloper.com

Game Developer is a leading resource for game development and industry news. The website includes links to its podcast on game development and interviews with those in the field. Additionally, there are blogs by people in the game development field, sharing what they are working on and offering career advice.

Game Dev Net

www.gamedev.net

This website provides tools and information on how to create your own games. It includes tutorials on game building, career opportunities, and blogs by those in the game development field. There are also spaces featuring users' portfolios of their games.

Women in Games

www.womeningames.org

This organization is dedicated to uplifting women in the video gaming career field. Its website provides access to *The Guide: Building a Fair Playing Field*, a resource book and inspirational narrative that is free to download. It also has information on its annual festival to promote women in gaming.

Programmer

What Does a Programmer Do?

Characters speak, a gun fires, and players level up in a game because of programmers. "I've made things explode, I made the camera move around properly, and I've made menus work,"[8] says Charles, a gameplay programmer at Ubisoft, a major video gaming development company. Charles fell in love with gaming and then learned how to program.

A game programmer gives life to video game design using coding languages such as C++, Python, and C#. The code turns ideas into an interactive experience with visually engaging environments, interesting characters, realistic or imaginative sounds, and narrative choices and outcomes. Programmers learn codes for various platforms, including computers, gaming consoles (PlayStation, Xbox, Nintendo), mobile phones, and tablets. Programmers use coding scripts (a series of instructions) within game engines to establish the game's elements and the way they will work together in the engine's environment.

As with game developers, the size of the company determines what type of work a programmer does. At a smaller company, a programmer

A Few Facts

Number of Jobs
About 174,400 in 2021

Pay
Median annual salary of $94,000

Educational Requirements
Bachelor's degree in computer science or related field preferred

Personal Qualities
Problem solver, innovative, detail oriented

Work Settings
Indoors, at computer

Future Job Outlook
Growth of 22 percent through 2030

Educational Advice

"Find yourself a good educational program. There is a lot of disagreement over whether to go for the two-year technical college program or the full degree. But I have always found that, when hiring, candidates with a four-year Bachelor of Science (or better) have been far more prepared with the mathematical and scientific fundamentals than people coming out of a two-year program. I find that the two-year programs focus more on project work and other work designed to pad out your resume. They are intended to get you hired, not to equip you with the scientific foundation you need."

—Dan Posluns, game developer and programmer

Quoted in Jason W. Bay, "How to Become a Video Game Programmer," Game Industry Career Guide, 2023. www.gameindustrycareerguide.com.

may be involved with coding all aspects of the game. At a larger company, programmers may specialize in various roles in the video game development process. Some may program visuals, others may be tasked with tackling a game's logic, and still others may work on coding the user interface or artificial intelligence that reacts to players' actions.

A Typical Workday

A game programmer's day is spent mainly at a computer, using hardware and software to work on a particular area of the game. Dimitrije Calic, a programmer at Ubisoft, works on developing game features and fixing errors, or bugs. Because Ubisoft is a large company, he is assigned specific features of the game to program. A feature might be a flaming sword, a character running, or a ball rolling. His job is to make the action involving a feature look realistic and smooth within the gameplay. "The most interesting part of my job is implementing a feature 'from scratch.' That's where you can see my personal contribution," explains

Calic. "Together with artists, designers, and testers, we have the creative freedom to shape the feature, to a certain extent. Seeing a feature that you worked on end up in the game is really remarkable."[9] If he finishes his task before the due date, he then helps his colleagues complete their tasks. Calic's days may include meetings with designers or other team members working on similar features, but most of it is coding, debugging problems in code, and solving other programming issues.

Like Calic, Dan Posluns is a programmer and has worked on top franchise games such as *Spore*, *The Simpsons*, and *LEGO Star Wars*. He has programmed on multiple platforms, including handheld and mobile devices. Because of his years of experience, he works on several features within a project. Posluns says:

> My days are spent implementing gameplay features, fixing bugs in existing features and systems, and working with artists and designers. I have to make sure they'll be able to use the features I'm developing, and that my solution correctly achieves what it is they want to do. That last part is important. A game programmer needs to understand the more ephemeral concepts that artists and designers come up with and translate them into concrete systems in code.[10]

Posluns believes that video game development is a team effort, so when he does his job, he is proud of how it advances the entire project.

Education and Training

Game development companies prefer that their programmers have an education specific to coding. While some will look at coding experience, a bachelor's or master's degree in computer science, information technology, or any related field gives you a better chance to get in the door at the company. "I have a [bachelor of science degree] in computer science and engineering, and an [master of science degree] in artificial intelligence," says Duygu Cakmak, who has been a programmer for over ten years and is now a project technical director at Creative Assembly, a game development company. "I think my education was closely aligned with what I wanted to do, and I would recommend a similar path to people who would like to follow a similar formal route in education."[11]

Programmers must know coding languages and understand how to use game engines, such as Unity and Unreal, to create the base architecture for each project. No matter a programmer's formal educational background, these skills are necessary. They can be self-taught using videos and programs found on the internet, or aspiring programmers can attend boot camps, short-term schools that teach these skills. While individuals do not receive a college degree from boot camps or other nonacademic paths, they will be able to show they have obtained experience and programming knowledge.

Skills and Personality

Technical ability is the highest priority for programmers. They need to be able not only to code the typical languages but also to quickly learn new languages as required. Programmers are also critical thinkers because their job is figuring out how to use code to make something happen in a game. Programmers are also continually learning the latest in programming and game innovations so that they are familiar with the ways coding techniques are evolving to meet new challenges.

The ability to calmly deal with problems is essential to the job because programmers are often confronted with a script that is not working as planned. If you wish to become a programmer, it will be your job to overcome such problems. "Different methods work better for different people, but keep in mind that there will *always* be a minimum amount of self-teaching that will be

> ### Programming for Programmers
>
> "My favorite part of being a tools programmer is that my customers are the people I work with, so I get instant feedback. I don't have to spend years working on a product and never know if people will like it. When I finish a task people stop by my desk to say thanks and sometimes even buy me cupcakes!"
>
> —Brian Gish, video game tools programmer
>
> Quoted in Jason W. Bay, "How to Become a Video Game Tools Programmer," Game Industry Career Guide, 2023. www.gameindustrycareerguide.com.

needed, since you'll be constantly running into novel problems frequently throughout your whole career,"[12] explains Rodrigo Braz Monteiro, chief technology officer at Chucklefish, a gaming company.

Working Conditions

Most programmers work on computers at a desk in an office. Some work remotely, and others go to a corporate building. Wherever they work, programmers have the most advanced hardware and software at their disposal. Programming is strenuous mental work, and companies know their employees must take breaks from coding. So, some companies provide gaming rooms where programmers and other workers can try out the latest games using different platforms.

Programmers at companies generally work regular hours during the week. When deadlines approach, though, programmers often work long hours and weekends to complete their assignments. They will remain working until they have fixed all bugs and the functionality matches the design requirements. Successfully marketing a game relies on meeting promised deadlines, so programmers put in extra hours to ensure the game hits its launch date.

While many may think programmers work on their own in front of a computer all day, video game programming is collaborative. Chris Lierman, senior video game programmer at Wargaming, a gaming studio, finds working with others beneficial to game design. Lierman explains:

> I enjoy working as part of a team. While it's very satisfying when I've completed a feature or game element and get to see it working properly in the game, it's an amazing feeling to see everyone's contributions working interconnectedly to create a massively complex system that can give the illusion of being its own little universe on screen. Working with a diverse group of designers, artists, programmers, musicians, testers, etc. can be a rewarding feedback loop of helping each other incrementally improve that little universe every day.[13]

Employers and Earnings

Outside of management positions, game programmers generally have the highest-paid positions in the video game field. According to the career website Zippia, the average video game programmer salary in the United States is $94,000. Factors such as experience, size of company, education, and certification affect how much a programmer makes. Among the largest game developer companies that hire programmers around the world are Nintendo, Microsoft, and Sony. Top-end earners can make over $134,000 yearly.

Programmers in larger companies can advance to become technical leads, lead programmers, or chief technology officers (CTOs). As they progress in the field, most programmers prefer to remain on the technical side because that is their passion. Monteiro says:

Most programmers are in love with their craft, and resist moving to more managerial positions later in their career. A typical path will involve becoming a senior or principal programmer, and many programmers will gladly stay in that position to the end of their careers, or they can become involved in more managerial roles and become lead programmers, technical directors, or CTOs.[14]

Future Outlook

As the video game market continues to grow, the need for more programmers will likely increase. And as the competition between game studios grows, programmers will be in demand to help advance the features and capabilities of the newest games. According to the Bureau of Labor Statistics (BLS), job openings for software developers, which includes game programmers, are expected to grow by 22 percent through 2030. If you love gaming and perhaps have started coding your own games, a career in programming might allow you to help construct the next big title.

Find Out More

Code Academy
www.codecademy.com
The goal of Code Academy is to help people gain technical skills, including computer programming. This website provides free online tutorials and quizzes to help people learn to code. Languages include but are not limited to C#, C++, and Python.

Game Industry Career Guide
www.gameindustrycareerguide.com
This website gives career information on many types of game industry careers, including programming. The site includes articles, interviews, and a link to a podcast—all focused on careers in video games.

SheCodes

www.shecodes.io

SheCodes is a nonprofit organization dedicated to encouraging girls and women to learn to code. The website provides free coding classes as well as success stories from those who are part of the field.

Audio Engineer

What Does an Audio Engineer Do?

When you play a video game, the soundscape helps create an immersive experience. Audible speech brings the characters to life, ambient sounds help make the environment realistic, and the musical score cues emotions and sets the mood. A zombie's groan, the wind whistling, and musical themes whenever a certain character appears are examples of the elements of a game's sound design. Audio engineers find or create these sounds and then enter them into the game engine so they play back at the right time. Essentially, game audio engineers create, design, and put into place the sound and music elements of a video game. And they must adjust the sound effects, ambience, voice, and music so that the right element stands out from the rest at crucial moments of gameplay.

Sound engineers work closely with designers to understand what type of audio is required throughout the game. Basic sounds—like a door opening or human footsteps—can usually be imported from a sound effects library, a database

A Few Facts

Number of Jobs
About 119,900 broadcast, sound, and audio technicians in 2021

Pay
Median annual salary of $52,080

Educational Requirements
Bachelor's or associate's degree in audio engineering or similar field preferred

Personal Qualities
Musical, technical, detail oriented

Work Settings
Indoors, in studios with audio equipment

Future Job Outlook
Growth rate of 10 percent through 2031

provided with the game engine or other software. If the engineers cannot find the sounds, they must create them. This process might require modifying existing sounds through audio software, or it might mean that engineers have to record the sound—hammers on an anvil, a waterfall, a helicopter rotor—in a studio or on location. Once they record these sounds, they incorporate them into the game itself through a mixing program in the game engine or via middleware, a program that adds applications to an engine.

Audio engineers use digital audio workstations (DAWs), specialized game audio mixing technology (which can be a stand-alone computer or a piece of middleware) to create and implement the sounds into the game. Audio engineers import the sound files directly into the game engine or into the DAW, where they can change pitch or volume, fade sounds in or out, and mix existing noises into new sounds for a specific gaming environment. The sound files are shared with the game programmers so that they know exactly what sound will be triggered at specific moments or by specific actions in the game. This collaboration helps the soundscape for the game to stay consistent and add to the reality of its world.

A Typical Workday

Audio engineers spend much of their days at their workstations mixing sounds. When needed, they may visit an audio studio to create sounds; they may even visit off-site locations to capture specific sounds, such as a car engine revving. Some audio engineers may oversee auditions for voice actors and do the recording and editing of these actors' speech.

During 2020 Sam Markowitz worked as an audio engineering intern for Activision Blizzard, a game development company that has produced popular games such as *Candy Crush Saga* and *Call of Duty*. He was part of the audio programming team working on *Call of Duty: Modern Warfare II*. His day started by catching up with emails and messages; then he would check to see whether he was assigned any short-term assignments

Coding Helps

"It's really a big plus if you learn to code. Not on a professional level, but enough so that you get an understanding of how it works behind the scenes (I started out learning Java and Unity). I have talked with many programmers and composers and both look at each other as magicians—meaning that they have no idea what the other one does, it 'just works.' If none of you have any idea of what the other person is talking about, this can get problematic once the deadline is approaching and the stress kicks in."

—Ted Wennerstrom, freelance audio engineer

Quoted in Jason W. Bay, "My Life as a Video Game Audio Freelancer: What I Wish I Knew Starting Out," Game Career Industry Guide, 2023. www.gameindustrycareerguide.com.

by managers. Next he would virtually attend any needed meetings. "I . . . have scheduled meetings with many different people on Activision's audio team, which includes the audio design team, who work on creating the sound experience of a game, and the audio programming team, who is in charge of creating and adjusting the tools that audio designers use,"[15] Markowitz explains.

Whereas Markowitz had a specific function on a sound team tied to one game, Chase Thompson, who has years of experience as an audio engineer, has the opportunity to explore more diverse aspects of sound design. Thompson has worked on game series such as *Halo*, *Fable*, and *Star Wars*, and he finds the variety of his days the most interesting. "My favorite part of my job is how varied my work is from day to day," explains Thompson. "One day I might be implementing game music for a new multiplayer mode, the next I might be fixing a bug with one of the vehicle sounds, and the next I might be helping design new and exciting technology with our programming teams."[16]

Education and Training

While not required, an associate's or bachelor's degree in audio engineering, sound production, or something similar can help an aspiring audio engineer obtain a job. Additionally, a degree in musical composition or a related field is an asset to someone who wants to compose and make music for games.

Whatever your background, you must demonstrate your proficiency with the technical skills needed to record, edit, and mix sound. A familiarity with middleware, including FMOD and Wwise, is important because these programs are the two most popular ones used by development studios. The middleware helps enrich the sound palette of a gaming engine, so audio engineers must also understand and be able to work with game engines, such as Unity and Unreal, because the soundtrack will ultimately have to function within these environments.

To become an audio engineer, you should amass a portfolio of work that shows that you can create music, mix and edit, use middleware, and implement sounds seamlessly into games. Another option to gain and show experience is to contribute to an open-source audio project or to compose the soundscape on your own or with someone else for a game demo. Also, if you are willing to work for free or at a low salary, obtaining a position as an audio engineering intern can help you get into the field and build a résumé.

Skills and Personality

This job requires a melding of technical skills and creative ability. Audio engineers use technology to produce sound effects, music, and voice-overs and to integrate them into the game software. "I think most people who don't already know about game development are surprised at how technical the job is," explains Jaclyn Shumate, who has worked in many different audio engineering jobs for games such as *Plants vs. Zombies* and *Fable: The Journey* since 2006. "You have to learn a wide variety of hardware,

Speech, ambient sounds, and music bring characters—and whole worlds—to life in video games. Creating or finding those sounds—and adding them to the game—is the job of the audio engineer.

software, and different techniques to create the audio and get it into the game."[17]

Audio engineers also need imagination and musical ability to create the actual music and sounds that bring the video game to life. They need a great sense of timing to be able to put the sounds and music in with the matching action in the game. For instance, they must match the noise of a character's footstep or a wolf howling to the image on-screen.

In terms of personality, aspiring audio engineers should be collaborative. They work with designers and programmers to ensure they are meeting game specifications and that programmers understand how to implement the music in the game code. Tied to that, they must be clear communicators so that they can share any capabilities or limitations of the sounds they create.

Musical Moments

"You're looking for just those key moments where you can inject a certain feel, certain type of emotion, and often they may be very specific. It may be like in *No Man's Sky*. First time you leave a planet after building your spaceship. So, it's just allowing the game to breathe and injecting those moments with a certain key emotion."

—Paul Weir, chief audio engineer for *No Man's Sky*

Quoted in Adam Murphy, "Why Sound Matters in Video Games," *The Naked Scientists*, January 21, 2021. www.thenakedscientists.com.

Working Conditions

Audio engineers generally work in a studio with equipment such as microphones, instruments, DAWs, specialized game audio middleware, and other hardware and software tools to create and edit audio content. They may work as in-house employees of a game studio or as freelancers, who contract to do work for different studios. It does not generally require travel, but the work may require some out-of-office trips to record sounds outdoors or at other locations.

The work schedule of audio engineers is often determined by what stage of the game production cycle they are in. Sound design might initially run on a standard nine-to-five schedule, but as deadlines loom, audio engineers might put in extra hours and work weekends. Working twelve-hour days during crunch time is not unusual.

Employers and Earnings

As of April 2023, according to Glassdoor, the average salary for a video game audio engineer was $52,080. As with other jobs, the size of game companies and the level of seniority affect salary. Audio engineers can be hired directly by a corporation or work freelance for different studios. Freelancers can work remotely from any location, but for those interested in joining an in-house team, major companies are spread across the globe. Epic Games in North Carolina, Sega in Tokyo, and Rockstar Games in New York City are but a few of the interesting locales for candidates.

Future Outlook

According to the Bureau of Labor Statistics, the job outlook for professionals working as broadcast, sound, and video technicians, which includes gaming audio engineers, has a predicted growth of 10 percent through 2031. With the gaming industry on the rise, more companies will need audio engineers to enhance their games and draw in people to play. If you love music, technical work, and video games, audio engineer could be a great career for you.

Find Out More

Audiokinetic
www.audiokinetic.com
Audiokinetic is a company that provides audio products, including Wwise, used in game development. Its website provides an online certification for Wwise, videos one can watch about Wwise and how to use it, and links to audio-related blogs.

Game Audio Network Guild
www.audiogang.org
The Game Audio Network Guild is a worldwide community of those in the gaming audio profession. Its website provides news about happenings in the industry, gives information about upcoming events, has online forums where users can connect, and includes a digital version of its seasonal magazine.

Game Sound Con

www.gamesoundcon.com

This website provides information on the annual Game Sound Conference, which people attend to connect and learn about the latest happenings in game sound. The site provides information on the conference as well as game industry survey results, information about people working in gaming sound, and a blog with various audio-related gaming information.

Game Animator

What Does a Game Animator Do?

If a character jumps, trees sway, or a rocket blasts off into space during gameplay, game animators were responsible for making that happen. Any action you see while playing is the animators' creation, and it is their job to bring the characters, creatures, props, and vehicles to life through movement. Tony Ravo, a video game character animator for games such as *Finding Nemo* and *Harry Potter and the Chamber of Secrets*, says:

> Being an animator is a cross between Dr. Frankenstein and an actor. We basically have to animate—which literally means "give life" to—static drawings or 3D character models. That's the Dr. Frankenstein part. The actor part is not just moving them around but giving them personality and purpose so the player cares about the character no matter how large they are on the screen.[18]

To develop the animation, game animators use 3-D animation software such as Maya. First animators

---

A Few Facts

Number of Jobs
About 35,990 special effects artists and animators in 2022

Pay
Median salary of $57,295

Educational Requirements
Bachelor's degree in computer art, animation, or a related field preferred

Personal Qualities
Imaginative, observant, patient

Work Settings
In a studio or home office

Future Job Outlook
Growth rate of 5 percent through 2031

may develop a 3-D digital representation of any object or character. They use software, such as Maya and 3ds Max, to manipulate vertices (points in virtual space) to form an object or character. Then, in the software, animators construct the "bones" of the object or character, representing the skeletal structure. This is called rigging, which allows the animator to give motion to the character or object using software that can position and reposition the "bones." When developing the rig, animators must think about how they want the object to move and where the joints or other points of articulation will be. Once the rigging is done, game animators create movements for the objects and develop libraries of all the movements they create. A single character, for example, might have specific movements for running, sitting, climbing, and throwing, and each must be animated by manipulating the rigging to simulate the proper motion. Then these motions are all saved into a library, where the animator can recall them for another game in a series or give them new features for a character in a different game.

An animator uses the controls in the software and moves the rigged objects like a puppet. An animator will use keyframes, or static positions, as anchor points in the fluid movement of an object or character. Sophisticated animation programs can fill in logical movements of a rig in between the keyframes. When that work is finished, these animations are imported to the game engine. In the game engine, a programmer and animator may work together to develop the functions that tell the game what animations should be playing based on what the player is doing. Animation is a long process, but ultimately the attention to detail is what brings the game to life.

A Typical Workday

As a lead animator, Tony Ravo finds that his day often includes collaborating with others as they develop the design and look of a video game. "I am the one that is in the meeting and working with the Art Director to help set a style, and working with designers to

Working Together

"I got to interview with people from all different disciplines, not just animators, and they all wanted to know how I would collaborate with them. There are just so many more opportunities to collaborate since the teams are so much smaller. Over the years at Vicarious Visions, I learned a lot about being an artist and game developer, not just an animator."

—John Paul Rhinemiller, game animator

Quoted in AnimSchool, *How I Became an Animator for AAA Games*, YouTube, 2022. www.youtube.com/watch?v=2QtYMVcKxkY.

find out what they need. I also work with producers to create the scheduling and tasks for the animation team,"[19] explains Ravo. In addition to working on his own animations to meet the high quality required, his job includes ensuring that every animator matches the style he and the designers have set.

Ravo's day also includes a meeting with programmers to confirm that the animation he and his team develop functions correctly in the game engine. Additionally, he works with testers to gather their feedback on the responsiveness of the characters in early trials of the game. Not only does the animation need to look good, but it must also move the way a player expects. The animator must tweak the animation if it is not responding as it should.

David Gibson, an award-winning animator with over twenty years of experience, became the lead animator on the game *Valorant* by Riot Games. When he joined the team as an animator, the game design had already begun, but only two of twelve characters had been animated. The lead animator left the company nine months before the game was to ship. Gibson took over the position, but then he and his team of six animators had to design,

All of the on-screen action that takes place in a video game—sword fights, car chases, even swaying trees and flowing rivers—happens because of the work of game animators. They do this work with the help of 3-D animation software.

create, and implement the animations for the remaining ten characters within that short timeframe. Gibson says the challenge of working quickly was compounded when the studio campus shut down in response to the COVID-19 pandemic. Working remotely, his days were spent overseeing, encouraging, and collaborating with the other animators; animating his work; and keeping everyone on deadline. He and his team spent long hours working on the project, but they met their goal. "It was actually like a really good experience now that I think back on it," he says. "I'm . . . so proud of that team and that game."[20] Since then, Gibson has been hired as the animation director at Sony's Santa Monica Studio and is excited to tackle future challenges.

Education and Training

A bachelor's degree in animation or a related field will assist anyone who wants to become an animator for video games.

Many animators also come from an educational background in the arts, such as illustration or drawing. According to Zippia, a career website, 80 percent of video game animators have a bachelor's degree.

Without a degree from a university, a prospective game animator has to be resourceful in demonstrating experience. You can show expertise in animation through completing specific classes, attending animator-specific schools, practicing on your own, and creating your own portfolio of projects you have worked on. There are several online courses to become skilled in programs like Maya, 3ds Max, Houdini, or Blender. You might even learn how to animate in game engines such as Unreal. Practicing with these tools and producing interesting animation will help advertise your capabilities.

Skills and Personality

Animation requires you to possess an understanding of human and animal anatomy to create realistic movement in characters. Good animators are also observant and focus on details to believably animate any object, from a tree to a car, so that players stay immersed in a game world. A key personality trait is patience. It takes months or years to bring all objects in a game to life, and an animator should have the patience to enjoy the process to get every detail exact.

While imagination and artistry are needed to be an animator, as with most careers in the video game industry, technical skills are required. Understanding the entire game development process and having basic programming skills will help animators excel in their career. "There's a technical side to character animation as well. Knowing the game engine pipeline is a very useful skill and we don't just create an animation and throw it off to programmers," explains Ravo. "We need to work with them and shepherd that animation and character through the pipeline until the end."[21]

Working Conditions

Most animators work in a gaming studio office or, if freelancing, in a home office. A typical office will include monitors, video game consoles, and software and hardware needed for animation. Much of an animator's day is spent using his or her equipment to create the animations.

Depending on the size of the game studio, animators might be part of a team, interacting with others to develop animations that work together. In smaller studios, animators may work independently as the sole animator. Typically, animators will meet with designers and programmers as needed, throughout the day. Like most game development jobs, the hours and time spent on work can be long when a deadline approaches, but many find this time exciting as they work to meet their goals.

Employers and Earnings

The Bureau of Labor and Statistics (BLS) estimates that in 2022, 35,990 special effects artists and animators worked in the United States, with game animators being a part of this category. In 2023, according to Glassdoor, the estimated annual pay for a game animator was $57,295 in the United States. Additionally, Glassdoor estimates that senior animators generally earn over $100,000. The state with the most employers of animators is California, the home to many hi-tech video game studios. However, there are independent and major development studios throughout the United States that hire animators.

Future Outlook

The BLS estimates a 5 percent growth of special effects artists and animators through 2031. This projection includes about 6,700 openings for special effects artists and animators per year. This estimate, tied with the expansion of the video game market, makes a promising future for those who are considering the video game ani-

Start by Making Connections with Other Animators

"Reach out to other animators in the industry for advice and they will be happy to help, just be aware not to ask too many questions and respect their time. We've all been there, applying for our first jobs, so we understand the difficulty of breaking into the industry and are happy to help others. I definitely wouldn't be where I am today if I didn't post my work online and reach out to people."

—Sophie Shepherd, an animator at Creative Assembly

Quoted in Hitmarker, "What a Video Game Animator Does and How You Can Become One," July 4, 2022. https://hitmarker.net.

mator field. Most who enter the field feel the satisfaction of knowing that their work has a big impact on the success of a game. John Paul Rhinemiller, a former animator at Vicarious Visions, recalls being a part of the entire development team watching a live stream of people playing the game *Warmind*. He and the team had worked on the game for such a long time that seeing it being played live was an exhilarating moment. "People experienced [the game] for the first time that we had been so hard at work for," Rhinemiller says. "Just to watch people experience it and get joy of it and have that experience . . . it's something I'll never forget."[22]

Find Out More

David Anthony Gibson YouTube Channel
www.youtube.com/@davidanthonygibson
David Anthony Gibson, a professional animator for over twenty years, has a YouTube channel devoted to the craft. On his channel he presents videos of his work over the years and discusses these animations.

Game Anim

www.gameanim.com

Jonathan Cooper is the author of the book *Game Anim: Video Game Animation Explained* and an award-winning animator of games such as *The Last of Us Part II*. His website offers YouTube videos of different animators discussing their work.

Khan Academy

www.khanacademy.org

Khan Academy is a nonprofit online learning site that covers various subjects, including computer animation. The animation section of the website provides video instruction as well as written articles and interactive quizzes about animation, programming, and drawing.

VR Game Designer

What Does a Virtual Reality Game Designer Do?

Have you wondered what it is like to climb Mount Everest? Without leaving your home, you can cross icefalls, scale the Lhotse Face in Nepal, stay overnight at a base camp, and then climb to the summit of the famous mountain. After that experience, you can pilot a spaceship in the distant future or play golf on the PGA Tour. All of this is possible with the aid of virtual reality (VR) games. Using VR headsets and different types of handheld controllers and vests, you can put yourself into these exciting environments. Virtual reality allows players to engage in sensory experiences and become physically immersed in a game. Players use their bodies to move, turn, reach, speak, and perform other actions that are interpreted by VR equipment and translated into those actions within the virtual game world. To create these interactive experiences, VR designers use software and hardware to develop 3-D environments and determine how players can function within them.

Like all game designers, VR game designers develop the plan for

A Few Facts

Number of Jobs
About 265,000 graphic art designers in 2021

Pay
Median annual salary of $74,687

Educational Requirements
Bachelor's degree in art or video game design preferred

Personal Qualities
Observant, dedicated, imaginative

Work Settings
In a studio with VR gear

Future Job Outlook
Growth rate of 3 percent through 2031

Inside the Virtual World

"I love the feeling of being inside immersive tech and creating objects, environments, and worlds for it. It's a very transformative medium. It's almost like LEGOs in a way—but once you've built the world, you get to be the figurine inside it."

—Kathryn Hicks, VR designer

Quoted in Mastered, "Meet Kathryn Hicks, VR Designer and 3D Generalist," June 10, 2021. https://join.mastered.com.

how the game will work, the game goals and rules, and the look and feel of the places, characters, and surroundings. What makes VR designers unique is that they also design how players can interact with the world within the virtual, immersive experience. They control what players see, hear, and feel with each interaction.

Because the eyes are telling the brain that a player is in motion within the VR setting even if the physical body may not be in motion, VR games can make users nauseated. VR game designers have to try to counteract this motion sickness by giving the brain cues to contend with the mixed signals. "Creating a consistent visual frame of reference, such as a horizon or cockpit, which reduces motion sickness by giving the brain something fixed to focus on" is one way to proceed, writes Edward Moore, a veteran user experience (UX) design. "Another is creating a tunnel vision effect while the player is moving forward, reducing the number of changing stimuli in their vision."[23] For VR game designers, part of the excitement and challenge is overcoming obstacles like this to make an exciting world for players to enter.

A Typical Workday

VR game designers spend their days creating the visual and storytelling aspects of a game, including the characters, plots, and worlds. They use flowcharts to show the different actions and results of player interactions in the virtual world. They develop a storyboard, which is basically a group of still images that represent all potential scenes in a logical order. Much of what they design must take into consideration how the player will navigate the world.

Some VR game designers may spend their days developing visuals and animation for the game, using 3-D modeling or animation software, and import these into the game engine. They may also test the VR elements in the engine to see and hear the world they have designed. Often, however, programmers are the ones building what the designers have planned. The designers will meet periodically with programmers to ensure that their design concepts are possible and the program is working appropriately.

Also, designers may spend time redesigning aspects of the VR game after it has been tested. As an example, when VR game designers created the basics of the sword-fighting VR game *Sword Reverie*, they decided the virtual sword-wielding should feel like it does in the real world. To achieve this, the design included programming the controllers to feel heavier when swinging the in-game sword. However, while realistic, this did not feel satisfying when played. The designers then worked with the programmers to redo that part of the game. "We wanted the swords to feel heavier before the user swings, but lighter/faster when you swing them," explains Leon Zhang, lead designer of *Sword Reverie*. "This speeding up motion makes the player feel more satisfied as if they landed a huge blow to the enemy. (Even though it's the opposite of physics in the real world.)"[24] For Zhang and other VR game designers, getting to see the design in action and then improve the gameplay to provide a better experience for players is a rewarding part of the job.

Education and Training

Because VR is a newer field, there is not a set route to become a VR game designer. While degrees in video game design, art, and anything related are helpful to get started, they are not always necessary to gain access to the VR field. What is necessary is that VR game designers show that they have expertise in storyboarding, illustrating, and 3-D modeling. They also must be able to use game engines such as Unity and Unreal, specifically understanding how they are compatible with VR devices so that they know what the programmers can and cannot do. They also should be able to show a deep understanding of how designing VR experiences is different from other game design practices, recognizing how the effects of different visuals, sounds, and motions affect people in a virtual reality space. Those interested in this field can obtain this type of expertise by attending coding boot camps for VR or looking for other educational opportunities in classrooms or online to learn such skills.

Skills and Personality

A VR game designer needs imagination to envision how to engage players in a simulated world and provide an immersive experience. Designers must be organized and detail oriented to keep track of the actions that players can perform in the game and the reactions from the environment when players perform the actions. For example, if designers intend for a player to swing a virtual golf club, they must design how it feels in the player's hands with the controller, what noise the club makes cutting through the air, and what the player sees directly and peripherally during the swing.

To make these things happen, VR designers need to be able to use the tools to design and create a video game with VR. They should be able to work with 3-D modeling and game engines and have some programming knowledge. Also, VR designers must be observant to create the illusion of depth, height, and width so that players perceive them as natural in the virtual setting. "VR deals with 3D, tangible, and physical experiences," explains Zhang. "Therefore, either from architecture, 3D modeling, industrial design, or a *Minecraft* creative expert like myself, having great spatial awareness will be very helpful when designing."[25]

VR game designers create the visual and storytelling aspects of a game, including the characters, plots, and worlds. Designers also work with programmers to make sure their design ideas are successful.

VR designers must be problem solvers and creative in finding solutions. VR is still a new field, so designers will often run into unique issues. "That means the problems you are trying to solve in VR will often be something no one has ever dealt with," Zhang says. "If you are not an expert on the design process yet, you might struggle with how to make a good data-driven or user-centered design decision in VR."[26]

Working Conditions

Most VR designers work in a studio with their artistic tools, such as whiteboards, sketches, and computer drawing programs. They may use software for storyboarding, 3-D modeling, and animation. They will have access to a game engine and its VR components. They use VR headsets and controllers to interact with the games they are designing.

Design and Test

"When we build *Half-Life*, we just build it one piece at a time . . . conceptually one '*room*' at a time. And for each room a group of people sit there and they think: 'what happens in this room that hasn't happened in any of the previous rooms and fits into where we're going with the next room?' And then once you're finished with that process and you're happy with it, you put it in front of some playtesters and see what happens, and you iterate on it, and then you go onto the next room."

—Robin Walker, VR game designer

Quoted in Ben Lang, "Valve Explains the Deceptively Simple Design Process That Made 'Half-Life: Alyx' Excellent," Road to VR, April 14, 2020. www.roadtovr.com.

Designers may work on a team with other designers. Throughout the day, in addition to their design work, they may meet with programmers, artists, and other designers on the team. Some designers work remotely and attend meetings online.

As with all who work on game development, designers' hours can become long as deadlines approach. At this point, they are expected to work until everything is complete. For designers, this means redesigning aspects of the game that are not working correctly and ensuring that the final product meets the initial goals and, most importantly, is fun to play.

Employers and Earnings

A VR game designer makes a median salary of $74,687 per year, according to Glassdoor. One of the largest employers is Meta, which acquired the VR company Oculus in 2014. Meta has since brought the Oculus Quest and Meta Quest headsets to market. Sony is also a major player in VR gameplay. Its PlayStation VR games and gear are popular, and two big-budget Marvel Comics titles, *Spider-Man 2* and *Wolverine*, are scheduled for release in the fall of 2023.

Future Outlook

According to the International Data Corporation, augmented reality (AR)—in which the game is interspersed with the actual setting—and VR revenues were $12 billion in 2020 and projected to climb to $72.8 billion in 2024. Of the VR and AR markets, 80 percent of the revenue is from gaming, as opposed to VR film and other industries. While it is still a small part of the gaming industry, experts believe VR will grow in popularity, particularly as the gear required becomes more affordable. This projected growth will lead to an increase in games and more jobs for VR game designers. It will also help support a 3 percent growth rate for graphic designers, according to the BLS. If you want to work with cutting edge technology and the most advanced games, you should consider VR game design.

Find Out More

Affinity VR

www.affinityvr.com

This website provides the latest news in virtual reality (including gaming), recent information about VR apps and games, and reviews of apps and games. It also provides information on the latest products available for gaming in VR and articles on careers available in the field.

Game Designing

www.gamedesigning.org

Game Designing is a website dedicated to helping aspiring game designers start their career by providing learning resources, career searches, and information from experts in the field. It specifically provides information on the basics of designing and creating a VR game, the key concepts to understand, and virtual reality games that visitors can play to see how they function.

Justin P. Barnett YouTube
www.youtube.com/channel/UC1yXfU3c2gXchdmscjvCmMQ
Justin P. Barnett is a VR professional who learned how to develop VR games through online videos and self-practice. His YouTube channel provides information about VR careers and design tips for VR games, including animating, using engines, and otherwise working with the technology.

UI Designer

What Does a UI Designer Do?

In a video game, when you click on a treasure box to open it or press on a flower to make it bloom, you are interacting with the user interface (UI). A UI designer is the creator who determines how players will interact with the game elements and what will result from these interactions.

The UI designer focuses on designing the interface in the most intuitive way so that the users can easily engage with a game and accomplish the game's goals. The UI designer creates the menus, buttons, notifications, and navigation panes necessary to make this happen. UI design involves arranging the visuals to guide the user throughout the game while keeping it visually engaging and providing immersive experiences. "A game UI isn't there to attract the player's attention," writes John Cheung, a freelance writer with user experience (UX) expertise. "Instead, it's there to increase playability and help to build the seamless, immersive experience that makes up the best games."[27] UI designers also create features that are meant to keep players invested in the game.

A Few Facts

Number of Jobs
About 58,900 special effects artists and animators in 2022

Pay
Median annual salary of $75,000

Educational Requirements
Bachelor's degree in art, video game design, or computer science preferred

Personal Qualities
Artistic, intuitive, observant

Work Settings
In an office with artistic software, hardware, and sketching tools

Future Job Outlook
Growth rate of 5 percent through 2031

These include progress bars, badges, and features that track what the players still need to achieve. This allows players to see their accomplishments and encourages them to continue.

To accomplish these tasks, a UI designer starts by brainstorming with the team of designers and developers to devise the overall goals and themes of the game. UI designers then use software such as Adobe Photoshop, Adobe Illustrator, or Adobe Sketch to propose the icons, buttons, and visuals players need to navigate the game. From this point, UI designers use software such as Adobe XD, Sketch, or Figma to create wireframes, which are layouts depicting the location, structure, and flow of the UI elements. UI designers may also work with developers to integrate the UI design elements into the game engine. Designers may use a game engine's UI editor or layout tools to arrange and position UI elements on the screen and adjust sizes and location to achieve the interface they think will work best. UI designers are also involved in testing so that they can redesign UI elements and interactions based on user feedback.

A Typical Workday

Ben Humphreys, a UI designer and programmer with Brace Yourself Games, works at his company on-site, so his day includes many in-person interactions with others working on the production team. At the beginning of a project, he focuses on meeting with the designers of the game. "I'll talk to the game designers . . . about the game's features, their order of importance and ask as many questions as I can," Humphreys explains. "From gameplay-specific things like 'Can the player be poisoned *and* have other status effects at the same time?', 'How many different building types will there be?' to more production-related questions 'What platforms are we aiming at?', 'What languages will the game be translated into?'"[28] He aims to understand all of this before going on to the next phase, which includes sketching out the items such as health bars, build menus, inventories, and other game assets.

Humphreys likes to get his initial UI designs into the game for immediate testing to see whether the interactions make sense to a user. He redesigns these based on tester feedback. At the same time, he is working with artists to determine the final visuals for his menus and interfaces, including the colors, typography, and style. After redesigning the features and adding detail to the visuals, he places them back into the game for more testing. This cycle continues until he, the testers, and the programmers are satisfied that the final versions are easy to use and visually appealing.

Education and Training

Many companies hiring UI designers require candidates to have a bachelor's degree in a computer field, but no academic program provides all the skills needed for a UI designer. According to BrainStation, a coding boot camp organization:

> While many employers may want someone with a degree, none will expect that degree to be in UI—for the simple reason that there's no such thing as a Bachelor's of User Interface Design. This also relates back to the fact that most people enter the field of UI design from either the design side or the development side, sometimes—but not always—through Bachelor's programs like graphic design, human computer interaction or interaction design; many others simply begin practicing design or development and pick up more expertise along the way.[29]

For this reason, no matter what your degree, if your goal is to become a user interface designer, you need to develop the creative and technical skills for the job.

A successful UI designer must sketch and create visuals using the appropriate software. If you are proficient in Photoshop, Sketch, or Figma and understand vector graphics (computer graphics created through the manipulation of geometric shapes), you likely have the basic skills needed. Knowledge of animation is not essential, but the ability to use it is helpful—especially in smaller companies, which tend to employ people who can perform multiple roles. Similarly, most UI designers do not code, but understanding some coding basics is valuable when communicating with programmers.

Skills and Personality

Being artistic and having a technical aptitude allow a UI designer to create and work within a gaming environment. UI designers need to be intuitive and able to put themselves in the users' shoes to understand how players will react to the visuals and the interface. "Layout, color, typography, and other design elements all come into play here," explains an article on UI design on the BrainStation website. "Making them look appealing is only half the battle; the other half is anticipating how users will respond to them, then deploying these elements to achieve a desired reaction from the user."[30]

Designers should also understand that players have certain expectations concerning where menus are typically located and what the standard colors associated with buttons should be to activate game functions. It is the job of the designer to work with such expectations and strive to keep the interface easy to operate. While innovation is appreciated in any job, UI designers must recognize that significantly undermining player expectations of where to find controls on the screen can make a game frustrating.

Working Conditions

UI designers work in offices with several high-resolution monitors and a powerful computer to handle the game engine and the required software for animating, wireframing, and designing prototype interfaces. Designers also usually have a graphics tablet like Wacom Intuos to create digital or hand-drawn visuals. They

> ## Know the Engine
>
> "Often you'll have a dedicated programmer to do all the heavy lifting, but not always. From . . . proprietary systems . . . to modern staples like Unity & Unreal, you should know *something* about the engines that drive your work, particularly their limits and impossibilities."
>
> —John Burnett, UI art director and video game UI artist career coach
>
> John Burnett, "A Crash-Course in Getting into Video Game UI and UX Design for Absolute Beginners," The Wingless, June 23, 2020. https://thewingless.com.

also likely have "old-school" physical tools such as pencils and pens, sketchbooks, and paper to draw out quick ideas. To test their work in the game, they would have access to headsets and consoles.

The size of the gaming company impacts what daily work is like for a UI designer. Anisa Sanusi, a senior UI designer at Roll7, a British gaming company, has worked for years on game development for different-sized companies. "The teams I've worked on have ranged from a small studio of 12 people and I'm the only UI/UX person up to a company [of] . . . 500 people, and I'm in a team of several UI or UX specialists including programmers,"[31] Sanusi explains. Being part of a team means designers have more feedback from other members about how the interface is working with other parts of the game design. As Sanusi says, if you work on a game alone, you are responsible for ensuring that the interface works at every step and must fix any problems that arise.

Employers and Earnings

According to the online salary tracker PayScale, as of April 2023 the average salary of a UI/UX designer was $75,000 per year. Earnings are based on the size of the company, years of experience,

Invisible Interfaces

"Good design, when it's done well, becomes invisible. It's only when it's done poorly that we notice it. Think of it as a room's air conditioning. We only notice it when it's too hot, too cold, making too much noise, or the unit is dripping on us. Yet, if the air conditioning is perfect, nobody says anything and we focus, instead, on the task at hand."

—Jared Spool, founding principal of User Interface Engineering

Quoted in John Cheung, "Game UI Design: Everything You Need to Know," CareerFoundry, May 12, 2023. https://careerfoundry.com.

location, and job responsibility. Moving up the chain, UI designers can become lead designers, lead artists, and art directors, for example, and improve their salary. Some notable companies for quality UI designs are Blizzard Entertainment, which created the popular *World of Warcraft* and *Diablo* franchises, and Naughty Dog, which produces the *Uncharted* and *The Last of Us* series of games. Exciting UI opportunities can also be found at smaller independent companies, where designers might have more opportunity to innovate.

Future Outlook

Within the growing video game market, companies try to outpace one another with the newest technology. UI designers are specifically needed to create interfaces that work with emerging platforms such as augmented reality and virtual reality. Also, because gaming companies want their games to extend to many devices, from consoles to PCs to mobile phones, UI designers will be needed to adapt the interface across these platforms. These and other technologies emerging will give UI designers new and challenging ways to hone their craft in a job market that is expected to grow by 5 percent through 2031, according to the BLS. If you are artistic, drawn to technology, and fascinated by the interactive functions of games, UI design might be a good career option.

Find Out More

Figma
www.figma.com

Figma is a user interface software. Its website provides a free tool to try the software. It also provides a link to an online community in which users share files they have created using the software. Additionally, there are templates to scroll through for UI ideas.

GameDesigning.org
www.gamedesigning.org

This website was developed for designers to share information about game design. It includes product reviews, listing of game design schools, career information, and articles on the different skills and knowledge required for game design.

Game UI Database
https://gameuidatabase.com

Edd Coates, the senior UI artist at Double Eleven, created this website as a free resource for video game UI/UX designers. It is an online database of games and their UI designs. It is easily searchable by designers who want to see other games in a specific genre or are examining different game styles.

Source Notes

Introduction: The Future Is Now

1. Quoted in Steffan Powell, "*Death Stranding*: Hideo Kojima Explains His New Game," BBC, November 4, 2019. www.bbc.com.
2. Quoted in Erin Gobler, "11 Video Game Careers for Gamers," The Balance, September 1, 2022. www.thebalancemoney.com.
3. Quoted in Marie Dealessandri, "How to Get a Job as a Programmer," GameIndustry.biz, November 1, 2021. www.gamesindustry.biz.

Video Game Developer

4. Quoted in Brianna Scott, "The Number of Black Video Game Developers Is Small, but Strong," NPR, March 20, 2023. www.npr.org.
5. Quoted in Scott, "The Number of Black Video Game Developers Is Small, but Strong."
6. Quoted in Game Industry Career Guide, *What Is a Typical Day in the Life of a Video Game Developer?*, YouTube, 2020. www.youtube.com/watch?v=vVlMHZYqJ18.
7. Quoted in Scott, "The Number of Black Video Game Developers Is Small, but Strong."

Programmer

8. Quoted in Digital Schoolhouse, *Careers in Video Games: Game Play Programmer (Charles, Ubisoft)—One Minute Mentor*, YouTube, 2020. www.youtube.com/watch?v=rXL0vuW8sHM.
9. Quoted in Ubisoft Belgrade, *Gameplay Programmer Position at Ubisoft Belgrade*, YouTube, 2021. www.youtube.com/watch?v=77ltH0koDk0.
10. Quoted in Jason W. Bay, "How to Become a Video Game Programmer," Game Industry Career Guide, 2023. www.gameindustrycareerguide.com.
11. Quoted in Dealessandri, "How to Get a Job as a Game Programmer."
12. Quoted in Dealessandri, "How to Get a Job as a Game Programmer."

13. Chris Lierman, email interview with the author, June 1, 2023.
14. Quoted in Dealessandri, "How to Get a Job as a Game Programmer."

Audio Engineer
15. Quoted in Endeavor, "Activision Blizzard: A Day in the Life of a Sound Engineering Intern," 2020. www.endeavor.thecrimson.com.
16. Quoted in Jason W. Bay, "How to Become a Video Game Audio Implementer," Game Industry Career Guide, 2023. www.gameindustrycareerguide.com.
17. Quoted in Bay, "How to Become a Video Game Audio Implementer."

Game Animator
18. Quoted in Jason W. Bay, "How to Become a Video Game Character Animator," Game Industry Career Guide, 2023. www.gameindustrycareerguide.com.
19. Quoted in Bay, "How to Become a Video Game Character Animator."
20. Quoted in Pierrick Picaut, *Evolve, Overwatch, Valorant Interview with Dave Gibson*, YouTube, 2021. www.youtube.com/watch?v=MG79soah7sE.
21. Quoted in Bay, "How to Become a Video Game Character Animator."
22. Quoted in AnimSchool, *How I Became an Animator for AAA Games*, YouTube, 2022. www.youtube.com/watch?v=2QtYMVcKxkY.

VR Game Designer
23. Edward Moore, "Designing VR Games Worth Playing: 6 Key Considerations," Toptal, 2023. www.toptal.com.
24. Leon Zhang, "How to Get Started with VR Design in 2023," UX Design, January 10, 2022. https://uxdesign.cc.
25. Zhang, "How to Get Started with VR Design in 2023."
26. Zhang, "How to Get Started with VR Design in 2023."

UI Designer
27. John Cheung, "Game UI Design: Everything You Need to Know," CareerFoundry, May 12, 2023. https://careerfoundry.com.
28. Quoted in James Rowbotham, "Quick Dev Insights #03—Creating UI for Games—Ben Humphreys," *Quick Dev Insights* (blog), April 6, 2022. www.gamedeveloper.com.
29. BrainStation, "Do You Need a Degree to Be a UI Designer?" https://brainstation.io.
30. BrainStation, "What Skills Do You Need to Be a UI Designer?" https://brainstation.io.
31. Anisa Sanusi, *A Primer to UI/UX for Video Games*, YouTube, 2022. www.youtube.com/watch?v=yoUYp6bo95I.

Interview with a UI/UX Designer

Rachel Geng is a UI/UX designer who has worked as an intern with Facebook and Gamebreaking Studios, and she has created her own game, *Starweave*, in collaboration with a design team. She attended the University of Southern California's Games Program and received a master's degree in game and interactive media design in 2023. The interview was conducted with the author by email on May 29, 2023.

Q: Why did you become a video game UI/UX designer?
A: I grew up drawing and telling stories. I have a great love for the interactive medium of games, and UI/UX ended up being a perfect intersection between my passions for visual art, psychology, and game design. When considering the design of interfaces, there's so much functional utility yet worldbuilding behind each screen; they greatly and subtly affect so very much about the play experience!

Q: Can you describe your typical workday?
A: Video game design is a lot of problem-solving. A typical day involves evaluating the latest issues to tackle, working with teammates to find the best path forward, and then making it so. After charting out new UX flows, drawing new UI assets, and implementing changes into the game engine, we seek out a new problem to solve.

Q: What do you like most about your job?
A: There's always something interesting, and usually a little silly, going on where games are concerned. We're serious game developers, but it's easy to laugh over a funny bug or unique design solution. After all, we're making experiences to entertain others. A great job is full of levity and passion as we, too, strive to make our players laugh and even cry.

Q: What do you like least about your job?
A: Because it's a young industry, game development can fall prey to its own passions. Developers work long nights and push themselves too hard because they want to see their games succeed, all while balancing moving parts between various teammates, all the way up to managers, publishers, and investors. Sometimes, with deadlines looming, it's tough to push something—[that is] often overlooked—like UI/UX through, let alone get enough sleep.

Q: What was the most distinctive project or task you've worked on?
A: Definitely my indie game, *Starweave*, a tactical rpg (role playing game) about teenagers coping with roles they feel ill-fit to inhabit, which is systemically designed to nurture the player's own ability to see things from the other characters' perspectives. I've always aspired to make games for the sake of empathy and making the world just a little bit kinder, and I'm happy I could be UI/UX designer, systems designer, and creative director to 60+ developers to make such a game come to life!

Q: What personal qualities do you find most valuable for this type of work?
A: Expertise in design is important but only half the battle. Someone who works hard, stays hungry for knowledge, and stays humble in what they don't know yet will go furthest of all. This is the sort of person who will not only be the greatest designer of all tomorrow but is the kind of teammate and friend I want to most work with for years and years to come.

Q: What advice do you have for students who might be interested in this career?
A: Break down what it is you are affected by in the games that you cherish: why is this screen so satisfying to look at? What makes this gameplay so gripping versus another title in the same series or genre? Be receptive and open to the excitements and observations of your peers, too! Games literacy will not only inform your tastes but sharpen your ability to be a critical and communicative designer down the line.

Other Jobs in Video Gaming

AI programmer
Audio composer
Backend developer
Cloud architect
Database engineer
Game designer
Level designer
Level programmer
Lighting artist
Network engineer
Producer
Product manager
Quality assurance analyst
Rigger
Server engineer
Sound designer
Technical support specialist
Tester
Texture artist
2-D artist
3-D modeler
UI programmer
UX designer
Writer

Editor's note: The online *Occupational Outlook Handbook* of the US Department of Labor's Bureau of Labor Statistics is an excellent source of information on jobs in hundreds of career fields, including many of those listed here. The *Occupational Outlook Handbook* may be accessed online at www.bls.gov/ooh.

Index

Note: Boldface page numbers indicate illustrations.

Affinity VR, 45
Amazon Games, 12
audio engineers
 basic facts about, 23
 earnings, 28–29
 educational requirements and training, 26
 employers, 29
 information sources, 29–30
 job description, 23–25, **27**, 28
 job outlook, 29
 personal qualities and skills, 26–27
Audiokinetic, 29
augmented reality (AR) games, 45

Barnett, Justin P., 46
Bay, Jason W., 12
Blizzard Entertainment, 52
BrainStation, 49, 50
Bureau of Labor Statistics (BLS)
 earnings of game animators, 36
 job outlooks
  audio engineers, 29
  game animators, 36
  programmers, 21
  video game developers, 13
  virtual reality (VR) game designers, 45

Occupational Outlook Handbook, 58

Cakmak, Duygu, 6, 17–18
Calic, Dmitrije, 16–17
Call of Duty: Modern Warfare II (video game), 24
Cheung, John, 47
chief technology officers (CTOs), 20, 21
cloud storage, 5
Coates, Edd, 53
Code Academy, 21
coding languages and scripts
 audio engineers and, 25
 programmers, 15, 18
Cooper, Jonathan, 38

David Anthony Gibson YouTube Channel, 37
Death Stranding (video game), 4
Developer Satisfaction Survey (2021), 13
digital audio workstations (DAWs), 24
digital streaming, 5
diversity
 programmers, 22
 video game developers and, 8, 12, 14

earnings
 audio engineers, 23, 28–29
 game animators, 31, 36
 programmers, 15, 20

59

UI designers, 47, 51–52
video game developers, 7, 13
VR game designers, 39, 44
educational requirements and training
  audio engineers, 23, 26
  game animators, 31, 34–35
  programmers, 15, 16, 17–18
  UI designers, 47, 49–50
  video game developers, 7, 9–10
  VR game designers, 39, 41–42
employers
  audio engineers, 29
  game animators, 36
  programmers, 20–21
  UI designers, 52
  video game developers, 8–9, 12, 13
  VR game designers, 44–45
Entertainment Software Association, 4
Epic Games, 29

Figma, 53
frames of reference, 40

Game Anim, 38
game animators
  basic facts about, 31
  earnings, 36
  educational requirements and training, 34–35
  employers, 36
  information sources, 37–38
  job description, 31–34, **34**, 36
  job outlook, 36–37
  personal qualities and skills, 35
Game Audio Network Guild, 29
game designers, 4
Game Designing, 45, 53

Game Developer, 13
Game Dev Net, 14
game engines, 18
Game Industry Career Guide, 21
Game Sound Con, 30
Game UI Database, 53
Geng, Rachel, 56–57
Gibson, David Anthony, 33–34, 37
Glassdoor, earnings of
  audio engineers, 28
  game animators, 36
  video game developers, 13
  VR game designers, 44

Half-Life (VR video game), 44
Humphreys, Ben, 48–49

International Data Corporation, 45
International Game Developers Association, 13

job descriptions
  audio engineers, 23–25, **27**, 28
  game animators, 31–43, **34**, 36
  game designers, 4
  programmers, 15–17, 19–20
  UI designers, 47–49, 50–51, 56, 57
  video game developers, 7–9, **11**, 11–12
  VR game designers, 39–41, **43**, 43–44
job outlooks
  audio engineers, 23, 29
  game animators, 31, 36–37
  programmers, 15, 21
  UI designers, 47, 52–53
  video game developers, 7, 13
  VR game designers, 39, 45

Jones, Neil, 9
Justin P. Barnett YouTube, 46

Khan Academy, 38
Kojima, Hideo, 4

Lierman, Chris, 20

Markowitz, Sam, 24–25
Meta, 44
Microsoft, 20
middleware, 26
Monteiro, Rodrigo Braz, 18–19, 20–21
Moore, Edward, 40
motion sickness, 40

Naughty Dog, 52
Nintendo, 20

Occupational Outlook Handbook (BLS), 58

PayScale, 51
personal qualities and skills
   audio engineers, 23, 26–27
   game animators, 31, 35
   programmers, 15, 18–19
   UI designers, 47, 50, 57
   video game developers, 7, 10–11
   VR game designers, 39, 42–43
Play like a Woman initiative, 12
PlayStation, 44
Posluns, Dan, 16, 17
PricewaterhouseCoopers's Global Entertainment & Media Outlook, 13
programmers
   basic facts about, 15
   earnings, 20
   educational requirements and training, 16, 17–18
   employers, 20–21
   information sources, 21–22
   job description, 15–17, 19–20
   job outlook, 21
   personal qualities and skills, 18–19
   UI designers and, 51
   VR game designers and, 41

Ravo, Tony
   on job of game animators, 31, 32–33
   on understanding entire game development, 35
Rhinemiller, John Paul, 33, 37
Riot Games, 12, 33
Rockstar Games, 29

Sam Porter Bridges (fictional character), 4
Sanusi, Anisa, 51
Sega, 29
SheCodes, 22
Shumate, Jaclyn, 26–27
Small, Catt, 7
Sony
   game animators and, 34
   programmers and, 20
   VR gameplay and, 44–45
sound effects libraries, 23–24
Starweave (VR video game), 56, 57
SweetXheart (video game), 7
Sword Reverie (VR video game), 41

Thompson, Chase, 24
training. *See* educational requirements and training
tunnel vision effect, 40

Ubisoft, 15, 16
UI (user interface) designers
  basic facts about, 47
  earnings, 51–52
  educational requirements and training, 49–50
  employers, 52
  information sources, 53
  job description, 47–49, 50–51, 56, 57
  job outlook, 52–53
  personal qualities and skills, 50, 57
  programmers and, 51
Unity, 9, 18, 26, 42, 51
Unreal, 9, 18, 26, 42, 51
UX (user experience) designers. *See* UI (user interface) designers

Valorant (video game), 33–34
Vicarious Visions, 33, 37
video game developers
  basic facts about, 7
  diversity and, 8, 12
  earnings, 13
  education and training, 8, 9–10
  employers, 8–9, 12, 13
  information sources, 13–14
  job description, 7–9, **11**, 11–12
  job outlook, 13
  personal qualities and skills, 10–11

video games, 4–5
video gaming, careers in, 58
Vincent, Dakota, 5
virtual reality (VR), 5
virtual reality (VR) game designers
  basic facts about, 39
  earnings, 44
  educational requirements and training, 41–42
  employers, 44–45
  information sources, 45–46
  job description, 39–41, **43**, 43–44
  job outlook, 45
  personal qualities and skills, 42–43
  programmers and, 41

Warmind (video game), 37
Women in Games, 14
Wwise, 29

Zhang, Leon
  importance of problem solving abilities for VR game designers, 43
  importance of spatial awareness for VR game designers, 42
  on redo parts of games, 41
Zippia, 20, 35

Picture Credits

Cover: Gorodenkoff/Shutterstock.com

11: Gorodenkoff/Shutterstock.com
27: Kosamtu/iStock
34: Gorodenkoff/Shutterstock.com
43: Kobus Louw/iStock

About the Author

Leanne K. Currie-McGhee has written educational books for over two decades and loves what she does. She lives in Norfolk, Virginia, with her husband, Keith, two children, Grace and Sol, and dog, Delilah.